LEBANON

in pictures

by CAMILLE MIREPOIX

VISUAL
GEOGRAPHY
SERIES

STERLING
PUBLISHING CO., INC. NEW YORK

Oak Tree Press Co., Ltd.
London & Sydney

VISUAL GEOGRAPHY SERIES

Afghanistan
Alaska
Argentina
Australia
Austria
Belgium and
  Luxembourg
Berlin
Bolivia
Brazil
Bulgaria
Canada
The Caribbean
Ceylon
  (Sri Lanka)
Chile
China
Colombia
Costa Rica
Cuba
Czechoslovakia
Denmark

Dominican
  Republic
East Germany
Ecuador
Egypt
El Salvador
England
Ethiopia
Fiji
Finland
France
Ghana
Greece
Greenland
Guatemala
Guyana
Haiti
Hawaii
Holland
Honduras
Hong Kong
Hungary

Iceland
India
Indonesia
Iran
Iraq
Ireland
Islands of the
  Mediterranean
Israel
Italy
Ivory Coast
Jamaica
Japan
Jordan
Kenya
Korea
Kuwait
Lebanon
Liberia
Madagascar:
  The Malagasy Republic
Malawi

Malaysia and
  Singapore
Mexico
Morocco
Nepal, Bhutan
  & Sikkim
New Zealand
Nicaragua
Nigeria
Norway
Pakistan
Panama and the
  Canal Zone
Paraguay
Peru
The Philippines
Poland
Portugal
Puerto Rico
Rhodesia
Rumania
Russia

Saudi Arabia
Scotland
Senegal
South Africa
Spain
The Sudan
Surinam
Sweden
Switzerland
Tahiti and the
  French Islands
  of the Pacific
Taiwan
Tanzania
Thailand
Tunisia
Turkey
U.S.A.
Uruguay
Venezuela
Wales
West Germany
Yugoslavia

Sheep provide milk, as well as wool, for the Bedouin. These animals, which are tied together to aid in milking, are of the Awasi breed.

PICTURE CREDITS

The publishers wish to thank the following people and organizations for photographs used in this book: Aramco World Magazine; Embassy of Lebanon; Inter-Continental Hotel Corp.; Middle East Airlines Airliban; Camille Mirepoix; National Council of Tourism in Lebanon; United Nations, New York; United Press International.

Revised Edition

Copyright © 1978, 1974, 1973, 1972, 1971, 1969 by Sterling Publishing Co., Inc.
Two Park Avenue, New York, N.Y. 10016
British edition published by Oak Tree Press Co., Ltd., Nassau, Bahamas
Distributed in Australia by Oak Tree Press Co., Ltd.,
P.O. Box J34, Brickfield Hill, Sydney 2000, N.S.W.
Distributed in the United Kingdom
by Ward Lock Ltd., 116 Baker Street, London W 1
Manufactured in the United States of America
All rights reserved
Library of Congress Catalog Card No.: 73-90809
VI Sterling ISBN 0–8069–1122–0 Trade   Oak Tree 7061–6063 0
1123–9 Library

A vendor of "kaak," a kind of sweetened bread, sets up his tripod stand on the beach at Beirut.

CONTENTS

LEBANON

— Major road

- - - Other road

—+— Rail

0   5   10   15 Miles
0 5 10 15 Kilometers

SYRIA

An Nahr al Kabīr

BUHĀYRAT
HIMS

Halbā

Al Harmal

El Mīnā
Tripoli
Zaghartā

Amyūn

Besharre

Al Batrūn

Plain of Bekaa

Jbail
(Byblos)

Nahr Ibrāhīm

Ghazīr

Baalbek

Jounieh

BEIRUT
Al Judaydah

Zahlé
Riyāq

B'abdā

'Ālayh

Zabdāni

Beit-ed-din

Nahr al Bārūk

Sidon

Jazzīn

Dūmā

Rāshayyā
DAMASCUS
Baradd

Marj
l'Uyūn

Qatanā

Nahr al Litāni

Tyre

SYRIA

Demilitarized
Zone

Bint Jubayl

ISRAEL

Al Qunayṭirah

Demilitarized
Zone

BOUNDARY REPRESENTATION IS
NOT NECESSARILY AUTHORITATIVE

MEDITERRANEAN

SEA

Nahr Abū Ali

Orontes

Range

Lebanon Range

Anti Lebanon Range

L e b a n o n

Mt. Hermon

Nahr al Ḥāṣbāni

Nahr al A'waj

INTRODUCTION

LEBANON, A REPUBLIC since 1923, has been one of the most important regions of the Middle East since Biblical days. As the homeland of the Phoenicians, the country was a crossroads before the time of Christ and it has been a meeting place of civilizations ever since. It has been a port of call and a place of refuge where different beliefs, languages and liturgies have confronted one another.

Lebanon, the only Arab nation that is half Christian and half Moslem, combines European and Oriental influences; a maritime nation since ancient times, it now seeks to improve its agriculture and develop its industry. Lebanon, land of rocks, cedar trees and locusts, laced throughout with archaeological grandeur, looks down from its mountains to the sea. As the international crossroads of the Middle East, it links the great cities of the earth to Beirut, its capital, with easy access by air. London is but four hours away, New York, a scant eight, while Paris, Frankfurt, Rome, Stockholm and Copenhagen are all reached in three to four hours.

In Lebanon's five provinces, Beirut, North Lebanon, South Lebanon, Bekaa and Mount Lebanon, there are towns known and beloved by archaeologists of both hemispheres. Among them are Trablos, Jbail, Beirut, Saida and Sur, whose familiar ancient names are still used more often than not—Tripoli, Byblos, Berytus, Sidon and Tyre, all of which were great cities in Phoenician times.

Various races of people later invaded and conquered Lebanon—the Chaldeans, Assyrians, Persians, Egyptians, Hittites, Greeks, Romans, Byzantines, Arabs, Franks and Turks, all of whose cultures left some trace. The Arabs left the greatest mark, although the impact of the Crusades was great—citadels were built then that are still used and traditions of that period are still upheld. The Crusaders came chiefly from France, Germany, Italy and the Low Countries, but all these fair-skinned invaders were called "Franks" by the Arabs.

In modern times an Armenian influx, due to Turkish persecution, added an important element to Lebanese life. Ties with France and with European culture were renewed in the years between World Wars I and II, when France held a mandate over Lebanon. The descendants of all these people, whose knowledge, talents, blood and common interest mingled, form the present population of Lebanon.

The Great Mosque at Tripoli dates mainly from the Mameluke period, but incorporates parts of the older Christian cathedral of St. Mary of the Tower. The minaret at the left, which is Italian in style, is believed to be the bell-tower of the cathedral.

Like a scene from the voyages of Sinbad, an underground river flows through this vast grotto in the Caves of Jeita.

The main grove of surviving cedars is at Besharre. Known as "Cedars of the Lord," these average 100 feet in height, and the circumference of some of them is from 40 to 50 feet.

I. THE LAND

LEBANON, "LAND OF CEDARS," situated at the eastern end of the Mediterranean, occupies an area of 4,015 miles—somewhat smaller than Connecticut or Northern Ireland. Actually it is only a tiny strip on the map of the world, bounded on the north and east by Syria and on the south by Israel. The strip is 156 miles long but only 31 miles wide. Djebel Libnan, its Arab name, means "White-as-Milk Mountain." Two ranges traverse it, lying parallel to the sea, separated from one another by the high plains of the Bekaa. Set geographically between three continents, Europe, Africa and Asia, with all of its length on the beautiful coast, it is a true Mediterranean country. Charles Corm, a renowned Lebanese poet has said: "Never in the memory of mankind has so small a land so vast a destiny."

Much of Lebanon's natural beauty is easily accessible—almost any city or village can be reached from the capital, Beirut, within an hour or two. Beirut itself is just about in the heart of the country, a lively, cosmopolitan city with an ancient history and a modern outlook.

SURFACE FEATURES

The coastline from Tripoli in the north to Beirut is rocky and often steep. South of Beirut are sandy stretches, especially in the vicinity of Tyre.

The peak of Sannine, visible from Beirut, is covered with snow for much of the year.

The first mountain range, the Lebanon, from which the country takes its name, rises sharply from the coastal plain, and follows the shoreline from the Syrian border in the north to the mouth of the Litani River in the south, attaining its greatest height (11,024 feet) in the peak of Al-Qurnat-al-Sawda. The Bekaa plain, a plateau 70 miles long by 15 miles wide, lies between the coastal range and the inland range or Anti-Lebanon. The Anti-Lebanon, unlike the Lebanon range, which is entirely within the Lebanese Republic, is partly in Syria. Its highest peak is Mt. Hermon (9,232 feet) of Biblical fame, which lies on the border with Syria, near the point where both countries front on Israel.

Terraced hillsides rise above the beautiful Bay of Jounieh, on the coast a few miles north of Beirut.

Near Besharre is the beautiful valley and gorge of Qadisha, whose villages on the edge of precipices figure in the works of Gibran.

Between the snow-capped ridges of the Lebanon and Anti-Lebanon ranges, the intensely cultivated plain of the Bekaa has served as a granary since ancient times.

RIVERS

The River Litani (the ancient Leontes), which flows into the sea just north of Tyre, is wholly within Lebanon and drains the southern part of the Bekaa. The Hasbani, which is one of the sources of the international Jordan River, rises within Lebanon. The Nahr-el-Assi (the ancient Orontes River) rises in the northern part of the Bekaa and flows northward into Syria.

THE CAVES OF JEITA

The Dog River (Nahr-el-Kelb) which supplies Beirut with its cascades of bountiful pure water, leads to a magic spot—the Grotto and Caves of Jeita, discovered accidentally by a hunter named Thompson in 1837. Stumbling onto the entrance and hearing distant rumbles within, he fired a shot from his gun. The echoes that resulted made him realize that there were vast chambers and a foaming river inside. Thompson was not believed when he

The Pigeon's Grotto is a rock formation in the cliffs at Beirut. Water-skiers gain an additional thrill from the sport by dashing under its natural arch.

told of his findings, and no exploration was made until 1873, when two engineers from the Government Water Supply Department decided to follow the course of the Dog River.

Equipping themselves with life-rafts held up by inflated goat skins, they started out, eventually reaching the entrance of a different underground cave with narrow and low-vaulted spaces. Their amazement knew no bounds as they entered a high-roofed hall (still travelling on their raft) and beheld fantastic icicle draperies hanging in various shapes. They saw other strange and beautiful arrays of stalactites as well as ice formations of unusual form on the river banks. The engineers, Maxwell and Bliss, continued their exploration into this natural wonderland, hidden from the world for so long. Hours later, after learning the secret of the river's source, they emerged to tell of their unearthing of the caves.

Later the Caves and Grottos of Jeita were visited by speleologists (cave experts), who went along with Bliss and Maxwell to verify the findings, and excitement waxed high when the discovery was made public. Not until recent years were sightseers admitted. Since then, Jeita ranks high as a Lebanese attraction—just 12 miles from Beirut on a winding coast road.

From the Cave of Adonis, in the side of a precipice in the mountains east of Byblos, the Adonis River or Nahr Ibrahim, gushes forth. Legend associates the cave with the handsome youth loved by Aphrodite, in Greek myth.

PORTS

The Port of Beirut, sheltered by a breakwater, is today one of the best equipped in the eastern Mediterranean. Its two basins, capable of berthing 10 large vessels, were joined in 1969 by a third basin costing 40,000,000 Lebanese pounds (about $13,000 U.S. at that time), which will now double the facilities.

The ports of Tripoli and Sidon have special importance, as the former is the Mediterranean terminus of the pipeline from the Kirkuk oilfield in Iraq, and the latter of the pipeline from the Saudi Arabian fields.

The Beirut International Airport at Khalde (a few miles from the city's heart) is modern in the extreme, possessing technical installations comparable with the most up-to-date jet airports in the world. Every day there are more than 100 take-offs and landings which is double the amount of 1965, while the total number of passengers visiting Lebanon has tripled since then. The airport has become an important and essential junction of routes linking the East and the West.

NATURAL RESOURCES

Lebanon's greatest natural resource is its geographical location near the junction of three continents, as a result of which the country has become a major point of transshipment and the commercial hub of the Middle East. The great number of tourist attractions and excellent climate, winter and summer, must also be counted among the nation's assets.

Mineral resources are not great—iron was mined until recently, but the veins are now depleted. Lignite (brown coal) is mined to some extent, and gypsum is abundant. A great potential source of energy exists in the country's swift-flowing rivers, notably the Litani, which are being developed for irrigation and hydro-electric power systems.

The gleaming white city of Beirut rises abruptly from the rocky Mediterranean coast.

In spring, melting snows of the mountains cause even tiny brooks to overflow, permitting these boys of the Bekaa to fish in what appears to be a flooded field.

CLIMATE

The climate of Lebanon is Mediterranean, similar to that of southern California or the French Riviera. There are four equal seasons: winter, spring, summer and autumn, with 300 sunny days a year. During certain months, one can swim in the sea and just half an hour later ski at an altitude of 4,900 feet. The climate is temperate all year through. In summer, the temperature seldom exceeds 90 degrees at sea level, or 68 degrees in the mountains, where cool breezes always blow. Between June and October, the beaches are golden and dry, and it rarely rains. The average winter temperature on the coast is 56 degrees, and rainfall is more plentiful then. Most of the rain falls on the coastal mountain range, the Anti-Lebanon being somewhat arid.

In winter heavy snow mantles the boughs of the cedars.

An unusual, close-up view of one of the beautiful Cedars of Besharre. Growing to an average height of 100 feet, some cedars have a circumference of as much as 40 to 50 feet.

FLORA AND FAUNA

The road from Tripoli leads to some of the few remaining cedars, through the village of Amium. On the way lies a small summer resort, Hasrun, overhanging the Valley of Qadisha. Besharre, where the poet Kahlil Gibran was born and brought home for burial, is in a beautiful setting—the Cedars of Besharre are one of the last traces of the gigantic cedar forests which covered Lebanon in Biblical days. King Solomon built his Palace from the wood of the Cedars of Lebanon. They cluster on a hilltop, forming a magic mantle of green, snow-covered in the winter, beneath cloudless blue skies. Some of the trees are over 1,000 years old. The cedar is the national emblem and is portrayed on the Lebanese flag. Near the cedars are ski runs and hotels, used both summer and winter for holidays. A 7,550-foot ski-lift has been constructed by the Government Tourist office, making the area a first-class winter sports area. In summer the pure air, gushing waterfalls and green valleys attract many visitors.

In the intensively cultivated coastal region, wild plants, which are not numerous, include poppies, tamarisks, anemones and buckthorn. In the highlands are stands of oak, fir, cypress and pine, in addition to the famous cedars. On the high Bekaa plain, which is nearly treeless, various wild herbs are found—mostly of the daisy and pea families.

Of large wild animals, bears and deer are sometimes found in the mountains; smaller species include polecats, hedgehogs and hares as well as squirrels and other rodents. A curious mammal of this part of the world is the hyrax, or cony, which is about the size of a house cat and resembles a rodent superficially—but is actually a hoofed creature whose nearest relatives, according to zoologists, are the elephants!

In the marshes, flamingoes can be observed, along with pelicans, ducks and herons, while the higher ground supports many smaller birds, such as cuckoos and woodpeckers; falcons, kites and other birds of prey are also to be encountered in the mountains. Insects, especially locusts, are common; and eels, bass and mullet are among the fish found in lakes and rivers.

In spring the Lebanese mountains are covered with many wild flowers. These flowers are one of the numerous varieties of the large daisy family.

Beirut is a unique blend of the timeless and the ultra-modern.

The business district of Beirut is one of the liveliest in the Middle East.

CITIES

BEIRUT

Rising like an amphitheatre on the hilly shore, against the background of the Lebanon mountain range, the capital city enjoys an ideal climate. Its 800,000 citizens have one of the highest standards of living in the Middle East; their city is a charming blend of old and new, of European and Arabic influences, of brisk commercial activity and relaxation. Their homes and businesses are minutes away from splendid beaches, half an hour from cool, green mountains.

Beirut has been a trading city since 1500 B.C., when it figured as one of the chief ports of Phoenicia. Conquered by Alexander the Great, it passed to the dynasty of the Seleucids, descendants of one of Alexander's generals. In 140 B.C., the city was destroyed by fire, and for over a century its name disappeared from history.

The Avenue de Paris in Beirut is a tranquil tree-lined promenade, overlooking the sea.

Cypresses and palm trees impart a typically Mediterranean quality to the many parks and private gardens of Beirut.

15

Well-known to world travellers, the striking Phoenicia-Inter-Continental Hotel overlooks St. George's Bay in Beirut.

New office and shopping facilities, such as the Starco Urban Centre, are changing the face of Beirut.

The Place des Canons, called the "Burj" by the Lebanese, lies in the heart of Beirut's business district. Beirut streets have both French and Arabic names.

The Goldsmiths' Market in Beirut is world-famous for the exquisite workmanship of the jewels in its many tiny shops.

Occupied by the Romans under Pompey in 64 B.C., the city was rebuilt and once more rose to prominence. Emperor Caesar Augustus appointed his son-in-law, Marcus Vespasianus Agrippa, as governor. The port was reconstructed and trade increased, but the jewel in Beirut's crown was its school of law which outshone the schools of Constantinople, Athens and Rome. The fame and beauty of Beirut spread far and wide and inspired the poet Nonos of Panopolis to call it "Goddess of the Sea."

Two earthquakes in A.D. 502 and 551 accompanied by a huge tidal wave destroyed much of the city. Then, in A.D. 560 a fire completed its destruction. What remained was, during the Arab conquest, occupied by Omar Ibn el-Khattab in 635. Rebuilt once more, Beirut was captured by the Crusaders and became a dependency of the Crown of Jerusalem in 1110. The Franks held it until 1187, and one of their governors, Baron Foulques de Guignes, built the large Church of St. John, later changed into the Great Mosque, the only surviving monument of that era. Conquerors came and went until the 15th century when the port was again reconditioned and ships once more began to anchor in Beirut waters.

The Lebanese Emir Fakreddin El-Maani made the city his capital between 1590 to 1634. He was responsible for pacts with Europe, for the establishment of consular agencies, and he restored the pine forests in the suburbs. After his death Beirut declined, but later regained its prosperity when the Ottomans acknowledged the city's supremacy over other ports on the coast. When French intervention in 1860 resulted in Lebanon's gaining self-rule within the Ottoman Empire, the city became the true capital of Lebanon and from that time developed in all fields.

The Place des Martyrs is the central square of Beirut, and in the middle of the square is a statue commemorating those who died fighting for their country.

A short distance from the rocky promontory of Beirut are excellent sandy beaches, where the city's residents can enjoy surf bathing.

TRIPOLI

With 180,000 inhabitants, Tripoli is the second city of Lebanon. Capital of the Phoenician Federation after 700 B.C., the city maintained its prominence under the Seleucids, Romans and Byzantines. The Arabs took it in A.D. 638, but it was reoccupied by the Byzantines from 685 to 705. In 1109, it fell to the Crusaders under Raymond, Count of Toulouse, after a long siege, but it later passed back into Moslem hands.

Modern Tripoli consists of two parts—the port district of El Mina, on a small peninsula; and the city proper, which is two miles inland, and is in turn divided into two districts separated by the Nahr Abu Ali, a stream that enters the sea east of El Mina. The great Frankish castle of St. Giles looms above the many picturesque small streets that wander off from the Place du Tell, the hub of the city.

Tripoli is important as a seaport and rail terminus, and since completion of the petroleum pipeline from Iraq, has added oil refining to its economic activity.

The minaret of a mosque rises above a narrow street in Tripoli.

18

The Sea Castle, a ruined fortification built by the Crusaders in 1227–28, still stands in the port of Sidon.

SIDON

Sidon (still called Saida by old residents) is a small city of 22,000, but is like a large fishing village in many respects, and its name in fact means "fishing." Christ preached a sermon here on one of his journeys. The Castle of the Sea, built by Crusaders in 1228, guards the entrance to its port. The ruins of the Castle of St. Louis, and the burial grounds with their catacombs and mosques are revered relics of Sidon's impressive past.

At Sidon fishing boats are beached against a background of minarets and towers.

Ancient Sidon, a leading city of the Phoenicians and often mentioned in the Bible, is today a small, bustling seaport.

Today Sidon is prosperous, due in part to its importance as the administrative hub of south Lebanon and as a shipping headquarters for the oil industry. From Saudi Arabia, petroleum arrives via the Trans-Arabian Oil Pipeline direct to Sidon where it is loaded on tankers and sent to refineries in Europe.

The old and new mingle in Sidon. The townspeople are lively and yet a serenity of spirit prevails in this progressive small city, where the past is always present. A few years ago in Sidon, workmen digging a foundation discovered an ancient tomb containing a female skeleton covered in precious jewels. For use on her voyage to the after-life, a bronze mirror, mascara and other beauty aids lay beside her, as well as a pure gold statue of Venus. Archaeologists tell us that she must have been a royal personage, so perfect is the quality of her jewels. From time to time, such finds remind the people of Sidon of their city's ancient grandeur.

Ruins of an aqueduct from the 2nd century A.D. *are among the antiquities of Tyre.*

TYRE

Tyre (12,000), built on a small rocky coastal promontory, which in ancient times was an island, is today a small, quiet city shaded by palm trees against the background of the sea. Its castles and cemeteries tell of its periods of greatness and bear witness to the skill of its artisans. Recent excavations have brought to light remarkable remains of a city paved with mosaics, and restoration of these is in progress.

It was Tyre's own King Hiram who supplied the 80,000 woodcutters, masons and brassworkers who built Solomon's palace and whose chief architect is remembered today for his skill and brilliance. And it was Europa, the daughter of a King of Tyre (in Greek myth) with whom Zeus fell in love—and fled to Europe with her and named that continent after his stolen princess. Although Tyre today is a minor port, the people of the town still bear a proud air, for are they not descendants of the Tyrians of old!

OTHER TOWNS

Beit-ed-Din, a charming mountain town a few miles inland from Beirut, is noted for its splendid Palace of the Emir Bechir, a showplace whose gardens bloom with white roses for much of the year.

Byblos, which claims to be the oldest town in the world (a claim made also by Damascus in Syria), boasts tombs, temples and ramparts from Phoenician days, although most of the town dates from the Middle Ages—a huge Crusader castle still stands there. Located on the coast 20 miles north of Beirut, Byblos today is little more than a large village. Yet it was at one time the commercial and religious capital of Phoenicia.

The palace at Beit-ed-Din, built at the beginning of the 19th century by the Emir Bechir II (1788–1840), is considered a gem of 19th century Lebanese architecture. The palace is now used as the summer residence of Lebanese presidents.

The richness of traditional Islamic design embellishes a chamber in the Palace at Beit-ed-Din.

Egyptian records show a brisk trade with Byblos as early as 2800 B.C. Byblos was a source of papyrus, the reedlike plant from which the Egyptians made a sort of paper, and in time the city gave its name to history—for the Greek word for book, "biblos," from which is derived our word "Bible," is none other than the name of the city itself.

Arcaded galleries look down upon a serene pool in a courtyard of the Palace at Beit-ed-Din.

At Byblos, the visitor can inspect this royal sarcophagus, carved from basalt, over 3,000 years ago.

Zahlé, with 33,000 people, is Lebanon's third largest city. About 50 miles from Beirut, on the slopes of the Anti-Lebanon, this flourishing resort and market city is known for its flowers, vineyards and cascading mountain streams.

Archaeologists say that this grave at Byblos dates from sometime between 2,000 and 3,000 B.C. The practice of burying the dead in grain jars has no exact parallel anywhere else on earth.

The massive grandeur of Baalbek draws a steady stream of visitors, both Lebanese and foreign.

This sculpture from Baalbek represents the Greek sun god, Helios, from whom Baalbek derived its former name of Heliopolis.

Wheat, poppies and twining vines—symbolic of Bacchus—are delicately sculptured in this detail from a doorway in the Temple of Bacchus at Baalbek.

Floodlights illuminate the stately columns of the Temple of Bacchus at Baalbek.

BAALBEK

Among Lebanon's many splendid architectural remains, Baalbek is remarkable. This small town in the foothills of the Anti-Lebanon, was a famous city in Roman times, when it was known in Greek as Heliopolis—"City of the Sun." It is generally believed that it takes its name from Baal, a Phoenician deity, and that the city was a religious seat before the Seleucid dynasty changed its name to Heliopolis. The vast ruins include an Acropolis (hilltop temple) and an early Christian basilica, imposing temples to Bacchus and Jupiter, and numerous lesser buildings.

The Court of the Altar in Baalbek was richly decorated on three sides with colonnades, of which only a few columns remain.

2. HISTORY

LEBANON, WHILE TODAY a young and modern republic, nevertheless is steeped in 5,000 years of history, for its territory corresponds closely to that of ancient Phoenicia. Its origin is practically lost in time; however, in the dawn of the first recorded events (around 3000 B.C.) a branch of the Canaanites of the Bible occupied what is now Lebanon. They were called Phoenicians by the Greeks and later the term Phoenicians became synonymous with Canaanite. About 1500 B.C. the main cities of Phoenician civilization were Byblos, Sidon and Tyre, each important in the maritime and commercial activities of that world of long ago.

Tyre was considered the greatest Phoenician city-state—its seamen ventured forth to establish the first business empire known to mankind, founding Carthage in the 9th century B.C. and reaching the Straits of Gibraltar some 200 years after, carrying on a continuous trade in marble, glass, bronze, highly prized cedarwood and silks and brocades, valued beyond gold in that era. It was the Phoenicians who are credited with devising the first alphabet of 22 consonants from which most ancient and modern scripts were derived.

THE PHOENICIANS' INFLUENCE

Historians are unanimous in their recognition of the influence of the Phoenicians in spreading civilization throughout the ancient world. Yet there never was a Phoenician state in the true sense of the word, because of jealous rivalry among the independent Phoenician cities, some of which surpassed others in fame and prosperity. Not one of them was strong enough to subdue the others and achieve unity in order to form a great state, although at different periods they formed federations.

In the Archaeological Museum in Beirut are sculptures from all the periods of Lebanon's long history. This relief of a ship (3rd century B.C.*) was unearthed at Sidon.*

In the barbarian countries they invaded, they occupied islands which were easy to defend and established markets to which merchants of the world flocked. They colonized part of Cyprus, Rhodes and the Aegean Islands, and worked the mines of Thrace before crossing the Black Sea (then the terror of sailors). They founded Tarshish, a great commercial colony, on the coast of Spain. The historian Herodotus tells that after reaching Greece, Italy and Malta, navigating at night by the polar star, the Phoenicians were the first people to sail around Africa. Starting from the Gulf of Aqaba they returned to Egypt, passing by the pillars of Hercules (the ancient name for the Straits of Gibraltar).

For a long time, beginning about 1500 B.C., the Phoenician city-states were under Egyptian rule, except for a period of Hittite domination. The Hittites, an Indo-European people living in what is now Turkey, extended their power southward into Syria, but were eventually overthrown and Egypt re-established its influence in Phoenicia.

Phoenicia extended as far north as the town of Ruad (ancient Aradus) in Syria, and was bounded on the south by Mount Carmel (now in Israel), on the east by the mountain chain of Lebanon and on the west by the Mediterranean. The high ranges which separated the Phoenician cities from the plains of the interior, and the Mediterranean sea at their feet, were the two factors which determined their maritime destiny. The ports of Byblos, Aradus, Sidon and Tyre ensured for themselves a dominating place in Asian trade. Sidon and Tyre were the most flourishing ports and acquired supremacy over the other towns along the coast.

Phoenician sailors were navigators with intellectual powers and adventurous spirits. They explored the Mediterranean, east, west, north and south and brought to European shores the inventions of their civilization. They were pioneers in naval warfare besides merchant sailing and directed their efforts toward the conquest of North Africa and Spain.

At Beit Mery, near Beirut, are many Roman and Byzantine remains, such as this mosaic dating from about A.D. 500.

The great Temple of Jupiter at Baalbek was destroyed in a series of earthquakes. Seen here are some of the surviving Corinthian columns of the peristyle, or colonnade, that formerly surrounded the temple.

The Macedonians under Alexander the Great overthrew Persia, and Alexander was welcomed by all the Phoenician cities except Tyre, which he eventually took after a 7-month siege. After Alexander's death, Phoenicia was the object of a struggle between the rulers of Egypt, the Ptolemies, and those of Syria, the Seleucids, until its conquest by the Romans in the 1st century B.C.

THE ROMAN EMPIRE

The Roman and Byzantine period lasted seven centuries and was the most prosperous; Lebanon became heavily populated, an important part of the Roman world. During this era Tyre was the metropolis of Phoenicia, Baalbek was endowed with its majestic temples, and later Christianity appeared and flourished.

THE MIDDLE AGES

During the Arab and Frankish periods, the former extending from A.D. 636 to 1085, trading in seaports lessened to the point of standstill. From 1095 to 1291, two centuries elapsed in a struggle between the Frankish and Moslem

Towards the 9th century B.C. Egypt fell into a decline, during which time Phoenicia enjoyed a period of great independence. Soon, however, the Assyrians became mighty, sought an opening on the Mediterranean and subdued the Phoenicians. By the 6th century B.C., the Chaldean Empire, with Babylon as its capital, held sway over Phoenicia. Then, from 538 to 333 B.C., the Phoenician states were under Persian rule.

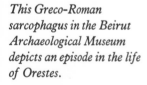

This Greco-Roman sarcophagus in the Beirut Archaeological Museum depicts an episode in the life of Orestes.

A detail from a mosaic pavement of the 5th century A.D., formed at Jnah, south of Beirut, depicts a variety of birds and beasts.

elements, mainly the Seljuk Turks and their successors. A new phase in Lebanese history came with the Egyptian Mameluke domination (1281–1516) when the Lebanese were kept in confinement within their hills. The old maritime cities of Phoenicia were occupied by rulers who collected duties without earning them, leaving the people to rule themselves, giving privileges to some and ignoring the rest. In this era, the Syriac language began to disappear and Arabic began to be spoken.

THE OTTOMANS

Syria was conquered by the Turkish Sultan Selim I (1512–1520), who put an end to the Mamelukes of Egypt. Selim did not attempt the conquest of Lebanon, but was able to exact

The great Crusader castle (left foreground) looms over the modern buildings of Tripoli.

tributes from the Lebanese Emirs (princely rulers). The native dynasty of the Maans, and later the Shehabs, sought to obtain greater autonomy for Lebanon and even total independence, hoping to unify all areas within the natural boundaries of Lebanon.

EMIR FAKREDDIN

The story is still told around hearthsides of the noble Emir Fakreddin who resisted Turkish rule and made history by building Lebanon into a land of strength and justice. From his palace at Deir-el-Kamar, he dispensed wisdom in spite of jealous enemies posing as friends. Fakreddin fell in love with a young and beautiful girl called Itr Allayl (meaning "Perfume of the Night") who, on behalf of the citizenry, presented him with a golden sword, while singing of her devotion. The romance of the Emir and Itr Allayl is still a popular subject of Lebanese legend and folklore.

Fakreddin ruled from 1590 until 1635. Although a Druse (see next page), he protected Christian interests, introduced European influences and even imported architects, engineers and other experts from Italy. In 1613 the Turkish army moved against the Emir and he went into five years of exile in Italy. After his return he succeeded in holding off the Turks, extending his power from Aleppo in Syria to the Egyptian border. The Turks at length succeeded in defeating him and carried him in chains to Istanbul where they executed him.

Though the Emir met a cruel end, his sacrifice was not in vain. He was never forgotten by his countrymen and the land for which he gave his life endures. In the Palace at Deir-el-Kamar his spirit lingers still, and in the legends of his countrymen.

BECHIR II

Of the successors of Fakreddin, the most distinguished was Bechir II (1788–1840), who temporarily succeeded in ousting Ottoman rule and placing his country under the protection of Egypt. During the period of Egyptian in-

Deir-el-Kamar, once the capital of the Emir Fakreddin, is a small town built around a central square, or "midan," a corner of which is seen here.

The 14th-century mosque of Taynal in Tripoli incorporates part of an earlier Carmelite church.

fluence, Bechir sought ties with the West. It was at this time that the American missions were established at Beirut and other places. However, in 1840 the Ottomans drove the Egyptians out and once more established a precarious control over Lebanon.

RELIGIONS

Internal strife had been developing between two of Lebanon's many religious groups—the Maronites and the Druses. The Maronites, a Christian sect, had been isolated from the main body of their co-believers, until in 1736 they became affiliated with the Roman Catholic Church, whereupon France declared unofficially that it would protect their interests. The weak Turkish government encouraged a heretical Moslem sect, the Druses, to oppose the Maronites as tools of a Christian European power.

During the period from 1840 until 1860, Maronites and Druses both rebelled against the government and also engaged in hostilities with one another. In 1860, angered by further European interference, the true Moslems joined the Druses in a drive against the Maronites, which resulted in a series of massacres of Christians of all sects. A French army invaded Lebanon and occupied it. In 1864 the Turks were induced to appoint a Christian governor-general for Lebanon and to grant the country a considerable degree of home rule.

The new régime was guaranteed by the European powers. Poverty was reduced, though many of the struggling citizens emigrated to new worlds and to Africa. The Turkish domination lasted until the occupation of Lebanon by the victorious Allies in 1918, at the end of World War I, and the country was occupied by France. Lebanon and Syria were later established as autonomous republics under French mandate. Lebanon, from 1918 to 1942, thanks to the new régime enjoyed a new way of life. The French mandate did not meet the wishes of the Lebanese for full independence, but had

The Church of St. John the Baptist at Byblos dates from the days when the old city was a Crusaders' stronghold.

Lebanese Christians throng to the shrine of the Virgin of Harissa, especially in May, the month of Mary. About 15 miles north of Beirut and over 1,500 feet above sea level, this colossal statue contains a chapel in its conical base.

THE PRESENT

Before assuming office, after being elected President in 1964, Charles Helou took the oath of fidelity before Parliament to the Lebanese nation and to the Constitution, in the following terms: "I swear by Almighty God to observe the Constitution and Laws of the Lebanese People and to maintain the independence of Lebanon and its territorial integrity."

Formerly the Minister of Education, President Helou (a Maronite) commenced his term peacefully, despite fears of possible violence resulting from pressures to re-elect his predecessor, and strove to uphold Lebanon's

certain benefits—with the encouragement of agriculture and industry, and the preservation of security, prosperity was restored. New schools were built and good roads and highways connecting the main points along the coast came into existence.

WORLD WAR II AND AFTER

In July, 1941, Allied forces took Lebanon from the control of the Nazi-supported Vichy French government. The Free French government, based in London, declared Lebanon fully independent. In 1943, the Lebanese elected their own government.

When the country was officially recognized by the United Nations in 1945, the Republic of Lebanon had come into its own. Strong ties with other Arab countries have been cemented while Lebanon maintained friendship with other nations. The history of Lebanon has been relatively stable since independence. One exception occurred in 1958, when rebel groups whose aim was to make Lebanon a closer participant in the Arab League were put down with the aid of United States intervention.

In 1958 an attempt was made to overthrow the Lebanese government. At the request of President Camille Chamoun, United States Marines were sent into the country to help maintain order, but were withdrawn in the same year. These departing "leathernecks" are receiving a last-minute offer from a local rug vendor.

democratic processes. President Helou had numerous crises to face. In September, 1966, when the nation's renowned Intra-Bank closed because of huge sums drawn out by other Arab states, he authorized the closing of all banks in Lebanon within 24 hours for a short period, to restore stability and maintain the confidence of the public. In June, 1967, he had to face the sudden Middle East War with Israel, in which Lebanon was not actively engaged, but which still has repercussions on all fronts. Discord in his Parliament often upset normal routines and he had, on occasion, to call forth deputies at midnight or dawn and sit with them in conference until agreement ruled.

Although situated in the heart of the Middle East trouble zone, Lebanon had been able to maintain a certain detachment in pursuing its own national aims, until 1968, when Israeli commandos destroyed a number of planes at Beirut Airport. Israel alleged that the attack was in retaliation for Lebanese involvement in the sabotaging of an Israeli airliner in Athens.

In 1969, the growing activity of Palestinian Arab guerrillas on Lebanese soil led to open clashes between them and the Lebanese army, and in the fall of 1969, the Lebanese cabinet resigned.

In 1970, Suleiman Franjieh was elected President, and faced an increasingly tense situation. Pressure from the other Arab states was mounting, and Israel had sent guerrilla forces across the Lebanese border again.

In 1973, there were an estimated 150,000 Palestinian refugees in Lebanon. The Lebanese have attempted to keep a tight control over them, not always with success. The continued activity of Palestinian terrorists and commandos, notably at the 1972 Olympics in Munich, led to stepped-up Israeli reprisals across the Lebanese border during 1972 and 1973.

Then in October, 1973, war broke out once more, as Egyptian and Syrian forces attacked Israel in the Yom Kippur War. Fierce fighting took place between Syrian and Israeli troops close to Lebanon's southeastern frontier. Lebanon did not become actively involved, however, even though Palestinian guerrilla attacks from within Lebanon led to renewed Israeli retaliation. Even after a cease-fire was effected, the attacks and reprisals continued well into 1974. Lebanon was torn between two fears—an Israeli invasion, if the Palestinians were not kept in check, and Syrian intervention if they were suppressed too severely.

3. THE GOVERNMENT

LEBANON IS GOVERNED by the President, who is Head of the State, and is elected by Parliament for a term of 6 years. The members of Parliament are elected directly by the people. The Cabinet is appointed by the President of the Republic and is responsible to the Parliament. Only after an interval of 6 years may a President be re-elected. No person shall be eligible for this office unless he fulfills the conditions of eligibility to the satisfaction of the Chamber of Deputies.

EXECUTIVE POWER

It is traditional for all Presidents in Lebanon to be Christian, while the Cabinet is traditionally headed by a Prime Minister who is a Moslem of the Sunnite sect. The five provinces of the land are administered directly by the central government. The President's executive powers are numerous. He may promulgate laws after they have been adopted by the Parliament. He supervises their execution and issues regulations to enforce them, but he may not modify or set aside their provisions. The President can negotiate and ratify treaties, which he may bring before the Parliament. He appoints and dismisses ministers and presides over national ceremonies. He maintains freedom of speech and the press.

Riyadh Solh Square in Beirut commemorates the first Lebanese Prime Minister to hold office after independence.

LEGISLATIVE POWER

The Parliament consists of a single house, the Chamber of Deputies, comprising 99 members, elected for a term of 4 years. Membership is apportioned among the religious communities, the Maronites claiming the greatest number, followed in descending order by the Sunnite, Shi'ite (Moslem), Greek Orthodox, Druse, Greek Catholic, Armenian Orthodox and Armenian Catholic communities.

CONSTITUTIONAL RIGHTS

With so many separate communities within its boundaries, Lebanon stresses civil and political rights in its Constitution. Personal freedom, free enterprise, and equal employment opportunities are all guaranteed. Religious freedom is assured, and each religious community may maintain its own schools, provided they conform to the educational standards set by the state, and do not give instruction that is damaging to other creeds.

FOREIGN AFFAIRS

Lebanon's foreign policy is a broad one, encouraging free enterprise. No distinction is made between national and foreign capital or workers. Taxation is extremely moderate and ideal conditions are offered to foreign investors. As a member of both the United Nations and the Arab League, Lebanon aims to preserve its independent identity, to be on friendly terms with Arab countries and to serve as a bridge between the West and the Middle East.

Beirut is the headquarters of regional activities of the United Nations—such as the Relief and Works Agency, which is responsible for the care of Arab refugees. The United States, which contributes approximately $23,000,000 a year to this cause, has always had traditional close ties with Lebanon and has assisted in the preservation of Lebanon's independence, integrity and the promotion of its economic development.

While a member of the Arab League, Lebanon has never been an active participant in the League's front against Israel. When Israel struck back against the Arab states in 1967, it is noteworthy that Lebanon was the only nearby nation not invaded. The more recent Israeli action in sabotaging the Beirut airport and the stepped-up guerrilla activity near the Israeli border brought Lebanon closer to the Middle East conflict. Yet, when Arab-Israeli warfare was resumed in 1973, the leaders of Lebanon again managed to avoid open conflict with Israel.

An office bloc burns in the war-ravaged streets of central Beirut during the civil war.

Batroun, where these cheerful boys live, is on the coast 35 miles north of Beirut, and is one of the most picturesque villages in Lebanon. Its houses are built of "ramleh," a stone found in abundance near the coast, and its people, mainly fishermen and craftsmen, are also famous for the manufacture of lemonade.

4. THE PEOPLE

A VARIETY OF GROUPS make up the 3,000,000 population of the Republic of Lebanon. Just about 50 per cent of the people are Christians, most of whom are of the Maronite sect, while the other half are of the Islamic faith.

The Lebanese people are mainly descendants of the Phoenicians, Greeks, Byzantines, Crusaders and Arabs who, at different periods, dominated the country. The national language is Arabic, although French is to be seen on signs and heard on every street. Many Lebanese are fair, though almost all of them have the dark eyes of the Orient.

Racial equality is natural among these folk of mixed descent and the shade of a man's skin is immaterial. The standard of living is high for the Middle East, especially in Beirut, where banking, commerce, shipping, industry and the pursuit of entertainment are part of daily life. Country life is tranquil and old-fashioned.

POSITION OF WOMEN

Young secretaries arrive at their respective offices, dressed in the latest fashions of the West. While nearby Arab lands seldom allow young women to work in offices, in Lebanon very high positions in radio, television, medicine and science (to note just a few) are held by

COUNTRY LIFE

In the coastal villages and mountain hamlets, the village folk of Lebanon often own a plot of ground and grow their own food; daughters go to school to learn to read and write. When that is accomplished, they are often hired out to more affluent city families. The monthly stipend which a girl earns goes to her parents. This has been the custom for a long, long time and is an advantage for over-large village families with too many mouths to feed.

The farmer's children are a happy lot. Weekends they stand on country routes where city cars fly by, headed for the cooler air of the hills, acting as astute salesmen all, with their baskets piled high, laden with delicious fruits, crisp green lettuces with loam still on the roots and all kinds of vegetables. They wait to pour the purchases in a bag for the city people who are pleased to buy just-picked produce at half of city prices. The fishermen too, stand by the side of the road with their catch, for which

This young woman is wearing the conical "tantour," a headdress worn by noble Lebanese ladies as late as the end of the 19th-century, and which resembles the graceful headdresses worn by European ladies in the 14th and 15th centuries.

daughters of families who, two decades ago, would have been shocked by a young woman working. The influence of the French in the early part of the 20th century had a great deal to do with this. French ideas, French culture and traditions and the practical methods of the French had a great effect in obtaining more freedom for Lebanese womanhood.

Where once the veil existed, it has now vanished forever. When occasionally women appear on city streets covered from head to foot in black *burqas*, revealing only their eyes, they are generally visitors from Saudi Arabia, Yemen or Kuwait who have come up with their oil-rich menfolk to shop and see the sights. In Lebanese villages, some totally Moslem, others totally Christian, it is seldom that one sees a lady in a *burqa*. Women in Lebanon enjoy the liberty of Western women.

This sturdy stone house is typical of villages in the mountains.

This farmhouse of the Bekaa features a "liwan," a room open to the outside through a large arch.

they find a ready market—in fact, the demand is often greater than the supply. A refreshing aspect of these transactions is the wit and charm of the vendors.

THE HEADMAN

The farmers lead a clan-like existence; in strictly farming communities there is always a headman, much like a tribal chief, to whom other farmers and villagers go in times of stress and need. Although the headman and the villager may belong to different sects, problems are pondered over with a personal approach, and solved. A large variety of Christian sects exist in Lebanon, including the Maronites, who are affiliated with Rome, and the Greek Orthodox and the Armenians. The Moslems include Sunnites and Shi'ites and the heretical Moslem sect known as the Druses.

A number of Bedouin—nomadic Arabs from the desert—are found in the Bekaa plain. Living in tents, they raise camels and sheep, and sometimes work as farm hands at harvest time. They are gradually shifting from their age-old nomadic life to a more settled existence.

Houses in the Bekaa plain are usually built of washed earth, since building stone is scarce in that region. The ladder leads to the flat mud roof of the house, which often needs repairs, as the summer heat causes it to dry and crack.

A Bedouin relaxes at the entrance to his tent.

While her little boy waits patiently on the back of a donkey, a village woman chats with a friend.

Wearing traditional desert costume, this Bedouin reflects the good-natured, hospitable aspects of the Lebanese.

RURAL DRESS

The apparel of villagers is charming and old-fashioned: the women wear loose ankle-length dresses tied round the waist with a cord, while men wear balloon-like trousers and loose shirts, much in the manner of the ancient Orient. Everyday clothes are gay cottons. For festive occasions, clothes are made of silks and shiny satins, with lots of braid for trimming. The girls and women generally wear head-scarves, often beautifully embroidered. These same ensembles are always worn when national folk plays are performed.

A kaak vendor passes a pair of gypsy entertainers on the beach. The girl dances to the music of her partner's "buzuk," a sort of two-stringed mandolin.

This man of the Bekaa plain sports a striking headdress.

40

The Place des Canons is the Times Square or Piccadilly Circus of Beirut, ablaze at night with neon signs and the lights of cafés, theatres and discothèques.

CITY LIFE

The life of Beirut is vivid and varied. The souks (markets) hold glitter that is rare. The food, flower and vegetable vendors have stalls piled high with many-hued products. On every street corner there are carrot-juice stands and the freshly squeezed, vitamin-rich liquid costs very little. In restaurants as lavish as in France, Oriental and European foods are served.

In the coffee houses, men spend their leisure time smoking the hookah pipe, while many a profitable transaction takes place also, for business is often carried on there. All business in

In the ordinary cafés of Beirut, which are patronized mostly by men, tea and coffee are served. Men come here to relax, to talk, to play cards or chess or dominoes (as these two men are doing), or to read their newspapers and to smoke the water pipe, or hookah.

41

Modern apartment houses rise above a street in Beirut.

Beirut is sealed with several cups of pungent Arab coffee, whether in the great banking establishments or on a café terrace.

Night in Beirut is a different world of its own, with cabarets, theatres and hotels offering entertainment to residents and visitors alike. The hotels range from plush castles on the sea along the Avenue de Paris to most inexpensive ones on Hamra Street. Flower stands are everywhere and flower pots on every rooftop, along with chickens, pecking for food in the city's heart. Beirut is fashionable, sophisticated, modern—but with a difference. East and West rub shoulders with aplomb and a homey friendliness exists, which makes the visitor feel he belongs. Sports and horse-racing are daily events. The world of Beirut is endless in its scope and variety.

FOOD

The food of Lebanon is noted for its richness and succulent variety—travellers come to Lebanon to eat as well as to do business. *Mezzé*, the native spread, is a gigantic selection of hot and cold hors d'oeuvres, ranging from piquant and spicy small salads to bean dishes (mashed and mixed with pure olive oil); zesty tiny meat balls with nuts; shrimps and sea-food

The fez, a hat style popularized by the Turks, is still to be seen on an occasional Lebanese, as on this man playing cards in a café.

chopped almonds and honey. Lebanese people prefer everything fresh and have not yet adopted frozen foods.

A quick lunch may be a slice of hot ground meat rolled with peppers and condiments in a thick piece of *khobez*, the Arab bread. Chicken is more than popular and the barbecued kind, ready to eat, sells like hotcakes in towns and villages. Local wines, which are excellent, go very well with all Lebanese dishes, and the drinking water is very pure.

HOSPITALITY AND HOME LIFE

An inherent part of Lebanese life is hospitality, bred through the centuries in homes both humble and rich. Visitors, whether strangers or not, are received into the warm intimacy of a Lebanese living room. Seated on the divan, they are immediately served a tiny cup of aromatic coffee, strong and freshly made, accompanied by Eastern sweets. Village homes,

This is not Lebanese smörgåsbord, but the famous "mezzé," a multitude of exciting dishes, each served on individual plates. Among the dishes seen on this table are stuffed vine leaves, shish-kebab, fried frog's legs, and "hommos" (a puree of chick peas with sesame oil), sea food, almonds, pistachios and liver.

tidbits that melt in the mouth; delicate, rolled, juicy vine leaves stuffed with rice and meat; sausage rolls in crisp hot pastry; these are but a few of the 49 dishes placed on the table, and taken as a complete meal. This is accompanied by *arak*, an alcoholic liquid which looks like plain water and turns milky white when mixed with water, which is the way it is taken.

Shish-kebab is a popular Oriental dish of skewered lamb cubes, green peppers, spices and onions. Arab bread—the round, hot, flat discs of wheat—supplements an Arab meal. Meals start with appetizers such as mashed chick peas in sesame oil, eggplant salad and *tabboule* (chopped tomatoes, scallions, parsley and wheat germ), plus stuffed grape leaves. Entrées, Middle East style, stress lamb, cooked in various ways, always served with rice. Desserts are rich: *baklava*, a flaky pastry, is filled with

This man takes a cooling drink of water from a "bre," a porous brown earthenware jug. These jugs are a common sight standing atop the pumps of service stations and in other public places, so that thirsty passersby may drink.

43

two storeys high and made of stone, are severe in lines but softened by a trellis for flowering vines and grapes. Wealthier homes show strong Italian and French influence, with tall windows and French doors of glass.

The tailor, the butcher, the baker and even a servant, when called upon, may be dining at the moment of call. Without hesitation, the guest, unexpected though he may be, is asked to join the table. To refuse is considered an insult and some slight drink or morsel is generally accepted. Because Lebanon has been primarily an agricultural land rather than an industrial one, thousands of Lebanese nationals have emigrated to all parts of the world, bringing with them the spirit of progress, energy, new ideas and the will to get ahead.

It is estimated that there are 1,500,000 people of Lebanese blood in other countries, mostly in the United States, Argentina and Brazil. Emigrants often return with hard-earned wealth to shower upon families and relatives (whom they have supported through their immigrant years). The ties are strong and many return to stay and to build a home and business, not possible in their early struggles.

MEN OF ACHIEVEMENT

Among famous Lebanese the most widely known is Kahlil Gibran, who wrote *The Prophet* (ranking second only to the Bible in total sales). Though his life ended in the New World, he was brought back to rest forever in the Valley of Besharre—where a museum dedicated to his life and work was built in his memory. Among the contemporary poets and writers of fame, there are Charles Corm, George Shehade and Fargallah Hayek. Dr. Michel Debakey, the famous heart specialist, and Danny Thomas, the television and film star, are Americans of Lebanese origin.

EDUCATION

In Lebanon today the literacy rate is 86 per cent, the highest in the Arab world. Schools exist in every mountain village and hamlet, as well as schools in the cities for foreigners who wish to learn Arabic. Of three main universities (there are 8 altogether), the American University of Beirut, founded in 1866, is perhaps the best known. It houses four faculties: arts and sciences, with 22 departments; medical sciences, including schools of medicine, pharmacy, nursing and public health; engineering; and agricultural sciences. Many noted leaders today owe their success to having been educated and trained at the American University.

Saint Joseph's University, founded by the Jesuit Fathers in 1875, has a law school, engineering and medical school, a special institute dedicated to Oriental studies, and a library containing 12,000 rare books.

Heavy snow lies upon the little town of Besharre, birthplace of the poet Kahlil Gibran.

A modern mosque adjoins the buildings of the College for Women at Beirut.

The Lebanese University stresses law, political sciences, art and statistics among regular courses. The statutes of this college have been handed down from the ancient Roman School of Law of Beirut, a background of which its students are proud. Attached to the university is the Sursock Museum, a treasury of sculpture, rare manuscripts and Oriental pieces of art.

Each mosque and church in Lebanon is not only a place of worship, but also of education, where classes are held for children who study the Koran or the Bible. Education is Lebanon's strongest line of fortification. (The country's armed forces number only 12,000 men.)

A touching sight takes place every October when school terms begin. Just by the Place des Canons in Beirut, in a small market place, children of all ages from lower-income families gather with their parents. They are there to buy school books, used but clean, at a fraction of original cost. From a café balcony, one may watch a scene of bargaining that would do credit to a film—hundreds of students swapping and selling books, those they have finished with and those they wish to purchase.

Armenian high school students, who are native-born Lebanese citizens, go to a school specially attuned to their background. While they study Arabic in school, Armenian is the language spoken in their homes.

45

School children of Beirut are taken by bus to Sidon and sketch with enthusiasm on the grounds of Sidon's castle by the sea—a good way for the youth of Lebanon to study their ancient history.

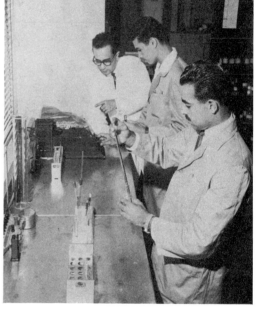

While receiving technical aid from other countries, Lebanon also provides aid. These Saudi Arabian students studying to become laboratory technicians are getting help in a chemistry experiment from a Lebanese professor in Beirut.

The painting class is enjoyed by children in this village school for boys only. In the strict Arab tradition, boys and girls study in separate institutions.

With snowy mountain slopes within easy reach, these young Lebanese have been skiing since childhood. The sun is bright and they do not have to be rich to enjoy it. It is a truly popular sport.

YOUTH HOSTELS

Lebanese Youth Hostels were commenced years before tourists came—when thousands of foreign young men and women discovered the country's forests, hills and river banks on hikes and camping trips. Their enthusiasm was so great, that it led to the creation of a Youth Reception Headquarters under the country's own National Council of Tourism—with headquarters in Beirut. Any Youth Hosteller from Lebanon or abroad may register and join in week-end trips to archaeological sites where lectures are given by professors on related subjects.

A special project called "Vacation Work Camps" is in full effect. Young people come in groups by arrangement, select a leader from among themselves and spend two weeks or more, assisting on farms, picking fruit, erecting farm buildings, aiding in geology exploration and other activities of benefit to the countryside. In return they are housed and fed free, and enjoy sight-seeing tours on off days so that it is not all work and no play.

MUSIC AND DRAMA

Music is heard everywhere and music classes flourish—a majority of Lebanese children start music lessons in kindergarten. At the age of 5, they perform at the school's concerts. Folk art is popular and many theatres are dedicated exclusively to traditional drama, consisting of romantic plays and dancing, in which all the magic of Arabian Nights comes to life in a

A young teacher and some members of her class enjoy the Mediterranean sunshine from the balcony of their classrooms. Balconies are a common feature of Lebanese schools.

From July to September every year, an International Festival holds forth at Baalbek. Lebanese and foreign companies present music, drama and ballet (seen here).

Lebanon looks East and West—at Baalbek, Lebanese performers play "Hamlet" against the background of majestic ruins.

passionate, breathtaking manner. Private enterprises and government tourist offices organize troupes of folk dancers and send them abroad to show other countries the song, dance and drama of Lebanon.

At Baalbek, folklore presentations are given, as well as the annual International Festival, an event which music lovers from around the world attend. This Festival was organized with

Traditional Lebanese musical instruments include (foreground) the "nai," or Oriental flute and the "daff," a small, tambourine-like drum; the string instruments are the "buzuk" (left), reclining against the "kanun", or zither, and the "ud," (right) a very ancient instrument whose strings are plucked with a sharpened eagle feather.

the idea of using the temple sites as a natural background—and the first Festival in 1956 was a great success, including French and English drama productions as well as symphonic music. The Festival annually presents ballet companies, philharmonic orchestras and leading stars of the stage. Among the guest performers, have been Margot Fonteyn, Rudolf Nureyev, the Bristol Old Vic players and countless other noted artists. The Baalbek Festival constitutes one of the world's most esteemed annual cultural events and tickets are sold out months ahead.

The Lebanese Casino, on the Bay of Jounieh, includes an ultra-modern theatre. Here a concert is in progress.

FESTIVALS

Aside from the Baalbek Festival, there are many others—festivals are part of Lebanese life and many are held throughout the year. Among them are: the Vineyard Festival held each September at Zahlé; the Arab Horse Gymkhana held in October, at Ablah in the Bekaa; the International Cinema Festival held in Beirut, late in October; the Festival of the Olive Trees at Koura, held early in November; and the Sea Festival and Boat Parade in Sidon, in spring.

Most of the year, Lebanon has special events: winter sports in December; the Christmas celebration and Mass and the lighting of the big Christmas tree in Beirut; the International Skiing Week at the Cedars in March; and in spring the Easter celebration.

ARTS AND CRAFTS

The arts and crafts of Lebanon are carried on by village artisans who were taught at their father's knee. Between planting the small crops for the family's food, each village boy learns the art of hammering brass; creating leather camel-seats, handbags and boxes in rare design; or making pottery in every form and in bright shades. Lebanese excel in the goldsmith's art and throughout the Bab-Idris section of Beirut one can see jewellers at work on intricate, exotic patterns. Every town has its special craft: Sidon, for example, is famed for

Lebanon has its own tradition of hand weaving— the same kind of loom has been used for generations.

the delicate workmanship of its bone-handled Jezzine cutlery. Throughout Lebanon, art exhibitions are held by young painters who study exclusively in art schools. Some specialize in painting the natural beauty of the local landscape, others follow the surrealistic trend.

At the weekly market held at Souk el-Khan, near Marjayoun in South Lebanon, a potter shows a customer his line of jars and vases.

Wicker chairs, seats, baskets and other useful and decorative objects—are crafted chiefly in South Lebanon and in the coastal strip from Beirut and Tripoli. This young man is framed by the products of his skill.

Kalamoun, a village near Tripoli, is celebrated for its delicately engraved copper work. This coffee pot and tray are good examples of local craftsmanship. →

In the Tailors' Market in Tripoli, master tailors follow the craft handed down to them through ← many generations.

The art of glass-blowing is believed to have originated in Phoneicia in the 1st century B.C. Today the craft is carried on mainly in and near Tripoli.

52

A tanker lies off Sidon, waiting to be loaded with oil from the Arabian desert.

5. THE ECONOMY

THE ECONOMY IN LEBANON, since the dawn of history, has always been based on more than merely extracting the fruits of soil and sea: trade has been a primary activity.

TAPLINE

A great economic resource in Lebanon is the Trans-Arabian Pipe Line Company with headquarters at Sidon. "Tapline," its name in brief, is a modern trade route of steel running across the Arabian Peninsula—across northern Saudi Arabia, Jordan, Syria and Lebanon. The crude oil transported via Tapline from the oil fields of Saudi Arabia to the Eastern Mediterranean

moves nearly 900 miles overland. Otherwise an oil tanker would have to make a sea voyage between the same two points that would be ten times as far, round trip. This tremendous short cut has brought economic gain and intense new development to the countries through which it passes.

The company's marine terminal, south of Sidon, has four deep-water berths offshore. Tankers of all sizes, flying flags from around the world, take on cargoes of crude oil for the final stage of transportation to Western European and South American markets. Completed in 1950, the terminal in the ancient

A close-up of the pipes at the Sidon terminus of the Saudi Arabian pipeline dramatizes the modern side of this age-old city.

Phoenician city of Sidon has infused new life, new prospects and pride into the community. There are 330 different types of jobs held by employees, each one trained to do his part.

The Tapline is a small world by itself, with excellent housing, schools, clinics and other facilities. Tapline directs its over-all operation from its main offices in Beirut.

In Sidon a unique method was devised to install 36-inch submarine pipeline. This 6,650-foot length of pipe, welded into one piece, was towed to sea from the shore and slowly submerged by filling it progressively with naphtha, then sea water.

INDUSTRY

Lebanon is expanding its facilities for industrial production. It now possesses abundant electric power, produced by hydroelectric installations; easier and faster communications provided by a well-kept highway system and enlarged modern seaports and airport, plus a growing body of skilled workers. To increase the working force, a well equipped technical school has been established at Dikwaneh in which all trades are taught. To increase industrial expansion, the State has exempted from taxation all enterprises contributing to the country's development. Long- and medium-term credit facilities are offered to encourage industrial progress by the Development Bank.

A new and thriving industry is the manufacturing and processing of noodles. The textile industry ranks high in importance, with products ranging from raw thread to finished silks and woollens. Clothing is now mass-produced and the shoes and handbags of modern design are of very high quality. Over 1,000 furniture factories flourish throughout this small land and many more are springing up. The Lebanese have a feeling for design and their leather, wood and paper products are in demand.

Chocolate is a speciality, most of it made in Tripoli, and exported, either as a sweet or in biscuits, put up in attractive tins. Many United States soft drink companies have huge plants in Lebanon. These plants have thousands of Lebanese employees and because of the warm Mediterranean climate, the volume of business is great. The bottles are also manufactured locally.

Stone-masonry and brick-making are also up-and-coming industries, as are plastic and rubber products.

Soap-making is a major industry in Tripoli. This serene structure is not a cloister, but a former Turkish army barracks converted into a warehouse for soap.

This handsome hotel, the Al-Bustan, in the hills of Beit-Meri, was built in memory of Emil Bustani, the Lebanese industrialist and financier, who built a commercial empire throughout the Middle East and Asia, and aided greatly in developing Lebanon's economy.

TOURISM

Tourism in Lebanon is one of the happiest sources of profitable activity—since the hospitality of which the Lebanese are proud fits them admirably for this line of work. The fascination of the country and the special kind of friendliness that the Lebanese have for visitors are overwhelming. Each year there has been a rise in tourism. The Middle East War of June, 1967, dampened the enthusiasm of some travellers, but not for long, and the National Council of Tourism works day and night planning new tourist facilities and improving existing ones.

At Byblos, fishermen inspect their traps. Fishing is an important economic activity on the Lebanese coast, and has been since Phoenician times, when Tyre and Sidon shipped purple dye, obtained from the shell of the local Murex mollusk, all over the Mediterranean.

The Bank of Lebanon is housed in this gleaming new building.

EXPORTS

Among the exports are live animals, fish, spices, leaf and manufactured tobacco, raw cotton, wool and animal hair, textile fabrics, floor coverings, chemicals, miscellaneous manufactured goods and last, but not least, precious stones, gold, art works and antiques. A great proportion of these exports are sent to the United States. Lebanon imports from the United States a huge amount of crude materials, machinery and transport equipment, iron and steel, tools, ships and boats, food products, unmilled wheat, rice, oils, fats, tobacco, beverages, general fuels and construction tools. These imports aid in the upbuilding of the many new plants and factories outside Beirut.

FINANCE

The banking system is noted for its flexibility. The Lebanese are natural money-makers. Their instincts for good business run in countless directions. Bank managers appear to have psychic powers, often cashing personal checks for strangers on presentation of a passport alone. The check almost always is good and the stranger later returns with his business to that bank manager.

Human interest, seldom expected in financial circles, is a fact in Lebanon's banks. Shortly after the Intra-Bank failed, the poorest among its depositors were paid off by the Lebanese Government, which assumed responsibility for the crash. Such losses can no longer occur, for a Development Bank has opened, designed to provide industrial and touristic institutions with help on long-range terms at low interest rates. This will strengthen the private sector and encourage more individual initiative. The Government's policy is to leave the field open to free enterprise. Their establishment of the Central Bank, some two years ago, has provided Lebanon with monetary independence, which assures full government backing to all commercial banks in financial transactions.

TAXATION

Income tax is light on both individuals and corporations. The greater part of government revenue comes from indirect levies. Lebanese residents enjoy one of the lowest income tax rates in the world. A family man, after deductions for children, education, medical and other numerous personal expenses, has to pay only 2 per cent on an income of 4,800 lire (the Lebanese unit of currency, 3.16 lire equalling $1.00). If he earns 8,000 lire, the family man pay only 3 per cent tax, with 10 per cent being the largest amount, taken above an income of 48,000 lire. This makes for firm economy and happy citizens.

COMMERCE

Commercial activity is high in this land of 88 banks, where exchange controls do not exist and foreign businessmen may remit whatever monies they wish to their homeland. The transfer of profits is free. Repatriation of capital is unlimited and foreign investors welcome the fact that in Lebanon their patents and trademarks have protection.

Lebanon has a first-class network of highways. Here the coast road from Tripoli to Beirut passes through the town of Jounieh.

Sheikh Najib Alamuddin, chairman of Middle East Airlines and descendant of a noble family, epitomizes the new leaders of Lebanon, schooled in the cultures of both East and the West.

These aviation students are using demonstration equipment in the Civil Aviation Safety Centre in Beirut.

AVIATION

A vital part of the Lebanese economy is air transport. In Beirut's Khalde Airport, the words, "Welcome to Lebanon" are blazoned on the walls. In the great halls of this almost new international airport, offices of world-wide aviation companies stand side by side with Middle East Airlines, Lebanon's own national carrier. Middle East has an up-to-date fleet of Boeings for its far-flung operations. The airline's network serves 36 countries in Europe, North Africa, Asia and flies throughout the Middle East.

WORKING CONDITIONS

Because the population is highly literate, skills are plentiful and tri-lingual workers and technicians are common. The average secretary in Beirut, male or female speaks Arabic, French and English and employee turnover is low. Maximum hours are 48 per week with overtime pay for more. The right to form trade unions is guaranteed by law.

The government is conducting a soil survey and irrigation project to increase farm output. These workers are planting an experimental crop.

The symbol of Middle East Airlines—a stylized version of the national emblem, the cedar of Lebanon— adorns the tail of each of these planes at Beirut's Khalde Airport.

A Chinese poultry expert from the United Nations confers with the owner of a modern chicken farm.

Modern, scientifically controlled farms, such as this, help make Lebanon a leader in poultry farming in the Middle East.

The Lebanese are carrying out an extensive scheme to replace the country's denuded forests. Here forestry experts inspect seedlings.

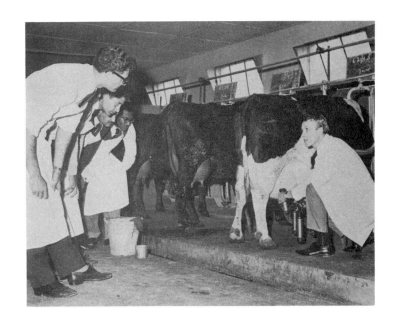

A Danish dairy expert demonstrates modern milking methods to Lebanese technicians at the Agricultural Station at Tarbol.

AGRICULTURE

On the great plain of the Bekaa, one of the foremost sources of Lebanon's past income was agriculture. Today, while yet a flourishing force, it counts for only 13 per cent of the economy, exactly equal to tourism as a source of national revenue. Yet agriculture continues to be one of Lebanon's principal activities, occupying half of the total population, and farm products are the major items. Despite its small area, Lebanon has a wide variety of landscape and cultivation.

More than one-fifth of cultivated land is given over to subtropical and temperate fruits. Apples head the list of fruits exported. Grapes are rampant in their growth and small country householders have vines rambling over wall and trellis. Olives and tobacco are next in value,

Under the Lebanese reforestation scheme, new access roads to timber lands are being built.

61

Age-old farming methods survive in rural Lebanon. This boy is threshing grain by driving over it in his sledge.

Sheep-farming is a main activity in Lebanon, since more mutton is eaten here than any other meat.

At Enfe, on the coast, windmills (seen through the blades of another mill) pump sea water into shallow enclosures, where it evaporates, leaving salt deposits.

followed by vegetables and cereals. Lebanon is sixth among the Mediterranean citrus-producing countries, with a production of 200,000 tons, half of this amount being exported, mainly to Arab countries, and to Eastern Europe.

Due to the range of climate, terrain and altitude, summer and winter fruits and vegetables are always available. Lebanon's agriculture is at present undergoing a renewal, known as the Verdure Plan, whose objectives are the conservation and improvement of the soil, the planting of trees to combat erosion, the provision of implements to small farmers, the training of qualified personnel and the placing at farmers' disposal of the financial resources required to develop their land.

The Government is also taking part in the financing of a navigation company, which transports Lebanese fruits in refrigerated ships. And to improve the balance of trade, an agreement is in effect between the Administration of the Verdure Plan and the U.N.'s Food and Agricultural Organization (F.A.O.) to survey new markets for further exports.

A village girl displays a huge sunflower head. The government is encouraging sunflower cultivation in depressed areas near Baalbek, whose people formerly gained their livelihood growing Indian hemp (cannabis), a crop that is now officially banned.

Dusk falls as this farmer of the Bekaa plain rides home on a bullock-driven sledge.

63

INDEX